Made in the USA
Monee, IL
13 March 2022

92880203R00061